MIND vs. MUSCLE

THE PSYCHOLOGY OF SPORTS

BASKETBALL

CATHLEEN SMALL

Gareth Stevens PUBLISHING

Please visit our website, **www.garethstevens.com**.
For a free color catalog of all our high-quality books,
call toll free 1-800-542-2595 of fax 1-877-542-2596.

Cataloging-in-Publication Data

Names: Small, Cathleen.
Title: Basketball / Cathleen Small.
Description: New York : Gareth Stevens Publishing, 2019. | Series: Mind vs muscle: the psychology of sports | Includes glossary and index.
Identifiers: LCCN ISBN 9781538225363 (pbk.) | ISBN 9781538225424 (library bound)
Subjects: LCSH: Basketball--Juvenile literature.
Classification: LCC GV885.1 S63 2019 | DDC 796.323--dc23

First Edition

Published in 2019 by
Gareth Stevens Publishing
111 East 14th Street, Suite 349
New York, NY 10003

Produced for Gareth Stevens by Calcium Creative Ltd
Editors: Sarah Eason and Jennifer Sanderson
Designers: Paul Myerscough and Simon Borrough
Picture researcher: Rachel Blount

Picture credits: Cover: Shutterstock: Dziurek; Inside: Shutterstock: A Lesik: p. 18; Aspen Photo: pp. 24. 26, 42; Fabrizio Andrea Bertani: pp. 7, 28, 38; Bogdych: p. 20; CHEN WS: p. 39; Creative Family: p. 12; Dotshock: p. 41; Dziurek: p. 22; Keeton Gale: pp. 30, 37, 43; Stefan Holm: p. 35; Matthew Jacques: p. 36; Richard Paul Kane: pp. 29; LevanteMedia: p. 21; Jacob Lund: p. 4; Audrius Merfeldas: p. 13; Chris Minor: p. 9; Oneinchpunch: p. 10–11; Pavel L Photo and Video: p. 11b; Plavevski: p. 19; Rawpixel.com: p. 45; A. Ricardo: pp. 1, 15; Pavel Shchegolev: pp. 25, 34, 44; Roman Tiraspolsky: p. 14; Dario Vuksanovic: p. 31; Wavebreakmedia: p. 6; Wikimedia Commons: Keith Allison: pp. 5, 9, 23, 32, 33, 40; Erik Drost: p. 27; Isafmedia: p. 17; Snyder, Frank R.: p. 16.

Printed in the United States of America

CPSIA compliance information: Batch #CS18GS:
For further information contact Gareth Stevens, New York, New York at 1-800-542-2595.

CONTENTS

CHAPTER 1

THE PSYCHOLOGY OF Sports

Playing sports requires a willingness to try. However, playing sports well requires **athleticism**. Being great at sports requires both of these things, along with an understanding of **mental strategy**. The best athletes combine athletic skill with a deep understanding of the game and the strategies involved. They know that athletic skill is only part of winning. To be truly excellent at a sport, athletes must train their brains to understand and put into play the strategies that can make for a winning team.

HELPING ATHLETES EXCEL

Psychology in general can help people better understand themselves. People visit psychologists to help learn why they react the way they do in certain situations or to learn strategies to deal with stress or frustration. For example, psychologists often teach their clients relaxation techniques to help them manage their stress levels. The same is true in sports psychology, except that it is focused on sports and athletic performance. Sports psychologists are trained to help athletes excel.

Whenever their training schedule becomes tough, athletes focus on their passion for the game.

ALL IN THE MIND

Metta World Peace: Shout-Out to a Sports Psychiatrist

Even though sports psychology has been practiced for roughly 70 years, until fairly recently, it was not always taken especially seriously. Athletes who have spoken publicly about their success with mental training have helped bring attention to this field of psychology. One such athlete is Metta World Peace (formerly known as Ron Artest), who helped lead the LA Lakers to a 2010 National Basketball Association (NBA) Finals victory. After the team's win against the Celtics, he publicly thanked his **psychiatrist**, Dr. Santhi Periasamy, for teaching him to relax, which he credits for improving his game.

The Lakers' Metta World Peace (far right) helped lead the team to a victory in the NBA Finals in 2010.

WHAT IS SPORTS PSYCHOLOGY?

To encourage the best possible athletic performance, players and coaches often turn to sports psychology. Some teams have a sports psychologist on staff to work with the team as a whole. Individual players may also choose to work with a sports psychologist on their own, outside of the team, to help better their game.

Sports psychology looks at how psychology affects sports performance and how participating in sports affects an athlete's **mental state**. Sports psychology techniques can be used to improve athletic performance and also to help with team building and athlete **rehabilitation**. Some commonly used sports psychology techniques include **self-talk** and **goal setting**. Sports psychologists work with players, teams, and coaches to decide which techniques will best help the team members, and the team as a whole, improve their game.

Coaches use psychology to help motivate players before a game.

Physical drills are part of preparing for a game, but so are mental drills.

PSYCHOLOGY IN BASKETBALL

Basketball is a fast-paced game of strategy and athletic skill, so the combination of athleticism and **mental agility** is particularly important. Basketball is also a team sport, so mental strategy is important not only for individual players but also for the team as a whole. Players must strategize their own moves on the court, and they also need to think about the entire team's performance. The best basketball players know that no matter how good they are on the court, it takes the entire team to win.

Coaches realize this, too. In fact, while there may be a standout, star player on a team, it takes an entire team of dedicated players to make a great team. Coaches consider the strengths and weaknesses of each player and develop a strategy for the team, which they hope will result in a game win.

IT TAKES A TEAM

A game cannot be won on the efforts of one player alone, no matter how good that player is. So while coaches will use sports psychologists to help each individual player develop their personal skills on the court, coaches will also carefully weigh the strengths and weaknesses of other players on the team and make strategic decisions based on the team as a whole. Sometimes, those decisions involve trading players to build a stronger overall team. Other times, they involve having a sports psychologist work with players on different areas to help improve the team's weak spots.

Coaches also develop what they hope are game-winning strategies. Once they have done that, they can use sports psychology techniques to bring out the best in their players. They establish a strong **motivational climate** and identify each player's **personality traits** to build team unity.

Dedicated players make up a strong team.

Steph Curry helped lead the Golden State Warriors to their 2017 victory over the Cleveland Cavaliers.

MIND VS. MUSCLE

THE GOLDEN STATE WARRIORS: 2017 NBA CHAMPIONSHIP WINNERS

In 2016, the Golden State Warriors lost the NBA title to the Cleveland Cavaliers. Despite the Warriors having a very strong team—including **MVP** Steph Curry—the two teams were neck and neck throughout the championship games. The Cavaliers won the first two, the Warriors won the second two, then the Cavs took Game 5, the Warriors took Game 6, and the Cavs clinched the title by winning Game 7. It was a sweet victory for the Cavaliers, who had lost the 2015 title to the Warriors.

In 2017, the Warriors were determined to regain the title. The team added superstar Kevin Durant, whom they knew would give them an edge over the Cavaliers. They also knew they needed to get past the ghost of the 2016 finals, where they had lost, even though many had favored them to win. The players worked to forget 2016 and stay present in 2017—and their strategy worked. The Warriors lost only one championship game to the Cavaliers and ended up winning the title 4-1.

CHAPTER 2

THE BASICS OF Basketball

Basketball was invented in 1891, and like many sports, it has changed over the past century. The general location, equipment, and basic rules have stayed much the same as they always have been. However, there have been minor rule changes over the years.

Professional games are played indoors, but pickup games are often played on outdoor courts.

THE LOCATION

A game of basketball is played on a court. The court may be indoors or outdoors. Professional, college, and even organized high school and middle school basketball games are played on an indoor court. However, informal pickup games of basketball are played on outdoor courts all the time, everywhere in the United States and elsewhere in the world.

Outdoor basketball courts are usually paved with concrete or asphalt. While their dimensions are often close to those of regulation courts, they are not usually exact. Indoor basketball courts have wooden floors, usually made out of maple. They are highly polished.

Regulation court size for NBA basketball courts is 94 feet (29 m) by 50 feet (15 m). International Basketball Federation (FIBA) courts are slightly smaller, though the difference is invisible to the naked eye. High school courts are much shorter, at only 84 feet (26 m), but they are the same width as NBA courts.

Each end of the court has a basket mounted on a pole and backboard. The baskets are mostly 10 feet (3 m) above the ground or floor. Sometimes baskets are shorter on informal courts used for youth play, but baskets for high school, college, and professional play are always 10 feet (3 m) above the ground.

The court is divided into two halves: frontcourt and backcourt. Frontcourt is the offensive area from the midcourt line to the baseline. Backcourt is the defensive area behind the midcourt line that extends back to the defensive area baseline. Once a team takes the ball over the midcourt line into the frontcourt, it cannot move it back into the backcourt.

Basketball arenas are large and can accommodate thousands of screaming fans.

On each end of the court, an arc is painted on the floor or pavement. This is the three-point arc. When players make a basket from behind the line, they are awarded three points instead of the usual two for the basket.

Within the three-point arc, there is a free throw line painted 15 feet (4.5 m) from the basket. This line is where players stand when taking foul shots, which are worth one point each. Between the free thrown line and the edge of the court (called the baseline), enclosed by lane lines, is the three-second area, which is sometimes called the paint (because it is often painted). If offensive players stay within this rectangle for more than three seconds, the ball is given to the opposing team. In the NBA, this rule applies to defensive players, too.

The corners where the lane lines meet the free throw line are known as the elbows. A common strategy is to try to be the first player to the elbow, which offers the team an advantage in offense or defense.

The markings on the floor of the court designate different areas important in game play.

On each side of the lane lines are painted areas known as the block. This area separates offensive and defensive players during free throws.

The free throw line is also the diameter of a circle on the court. The top of that circle (the half farthest from the hoop) is known as the key. Many players like to shoot from the key. A basket from that spot is worth two points, but if the player is open, it is a good place to shoot from.

Players also like to shoot from the corners, which is where the three-point arc meets the edge of the court on either side of the basket. Like the key, this is a good shooting position as long as the player is open.

THE EQUIPMENT

Very little equipment is required for basketball. The court needs to have a hoop and backboard at each end, but even the net that is traditionally found hanging from the hoop is not necessary—as long as there is a hoop to shoot a ball into, a game of basketball can take place.

SHOES AND CLOTHES

Good shoes are a must for a formal, organized basketball game. In fact, inappropriate footwear may not be allowed on an indoor court. Basketball shoes have soles that grip the highly polished floor of the court. They are often high-top shoes. For an informal pickup game outside, there are no requirements for shoes or uniforms. Without a doubt, players will perform better if they are wearing good basketball shoes, though.

Basketball uniforms consist of shorts and a jersey. Shorts are generally long, coming to about knee length, and the jersey is sleeveless. The two opposing teams wear different-colored uniforms. Often, the **home team** wears a lighter-colored uniform than the visiting team, though this is not always true.

Sometimes, teams will wear a third jersey. The teams have standard home and away jerseys that they wear for games, but if a team's jersey is very similar to its opponent's jerseys, the team may opt to wear the third jersey to make it easier to distinguish opposing players during the game.

Steph Curry has a jersey for playing at home and another one for playing on the road.

ALL IN THE MIND

Bringing It Home: LeBron James

LeBron James was under tremendous pressure in the 2016 NBA Finals. He had returned to Cleveland to rejoin the Cavaliers, and many thought he was the team's hope for finally clinching an NBA title. The city of Cleveland had not won a pro sports championship since the Browns won the Super Bowl in 1964, and the city was dying for a shot at the spotlight.

James's Cavaliers teammate, Richard Jefferson, explained the pressure James faced: "I can't think of too many players who have put that type of pressure on themselves and then have delivered more times than not. And he embraces it ... He's doing this for his teammates. He's doing it for everyone, and that's a pressure that I know I couldn't personally handle. I have a tremendous amount of respect for him taking that on." Under that tremendous pressure, James and the Cavaliers became the 2016 NBA champions—and the city of Cleveland rejoiced!

LeBron James stands out as one of the sport's true stars on the court.

BASKETBALL IN THE EARLY YEARS

Basketball is a young sport. It was invented just over a century ago, in 1891. Back then, peach baskets were used in place of basketball hoops, and the ball was similar to a soccer ball. Dr. James Naismith, a physical education instructor, created the game to give athletes in chilly Massachusetts something to play during the cold winter months. He also wanted athletes to be able to play a sport where injuries would be less common than in football.

In Dr. Naismith's original game, there were 9 players on each team, and there were just 13 rules to follow. The rules were similar to the rules in basketball today, although, of course, now there are many more rules in the official game (more than 100). In the past, players couldn't run while holding the ball; they had to throw it from the spot where they caught it. They had to hold the ball in their hands, not in their arms or against their body. Points were scored when the ball was thrown into the peach basket and remained there. However, in the early days, it was just a single point, whereas, now a basket earns two points. The team that scored the most points would be the winner.

The first basketball teams were formed more than 100 years ago.

Although men's basketball tends to get more attention than women's, there are professional women's teams worldwide.

There were fouling rules, too. Players could not push, trip, strike, shoulder, or hold an opposing player in any way, and they also could not strike the ball with their fists.

Over time, foul rules became more defined. Baskets changed from peach baskets to rims, then to rims with nets. Backboards were added behind the hoops and nets. The team size changed from 9 to 5, although in experimenting with team sizes, there were at times as many as 50 players on a team. Soccer-type balls were replaced with lighter rubber balls that had the laces concealed. It was found that the exposed laces on soccer-type balls made dribbling difficult.

Dribbling was added as permissible, too. It was not allowed in the original rules of the game, but single dribbles (a single bounce before passing) were allowed in 1901, and then in 1909, continuous dribbling was allowed.

Finally, the points changed to the current standard of two points per basket made, one point per free throw made, and three points for a basket made outside the three-point arc.

CHAPTER 3

OVERALL TEAM Strength

Any basketball team is likely to have a couple of players that stand out as a truly exceptional athletes. However, a team is more than just one or two players. A good team is all of the players working together, improving their weak points and continuing to play to their strong points. Good coaches can use sports psychology to make their team work together like a well-oiled machine.

ENCOURAGING MENTAL TOUGHNESS

To bring a team together, coaches must encourage mental toughness in all players. In the field of sports psychology, mental toughness is a set of four characteristics that players who consistently play at top level have. These four characteristics are: self-confidence, internal motivation, focus, and the ability to perform under pressure.

Self-confidence is crucial in succeeding at anything. People who believe in themselves and their abilities nearly always outperform those who are filled with self-doubt.

Many basketball players tend to be self-confident and highly focused.

The same is true on the basketball court. Players with self-confidence believe that they have the ability to play well, and that confidence results in them playing at a high level. At times, self-confidence can be mistaken for cockiness or overconfidence, but there is a fine line between the two. Cocky players adopt an arrogant attitude about their skills, and overconfident players tend to believe that they are capable of much more than they are. Self-confident players are secure in the knowledge that they have strong aptitude in certain areas of play, and that if they put their mind to it, they can excell on the court.

Some basketball players are motivated by external **factors**, such as fame or money. They are motivated by the rewards that will come to them if they excel—whether those rewards are financial or attention-based. External factors can be motivating, but internal factors are even more so. The players who are motivated by something inside them tend to be the most mentally tough players.

NBA star Kobe Bryant played his entire 20-year career for the Lakers. He believes that part of his success is due to continually improving his attitude toward his game and building his self-confidence.

Internal motivation is often a desire for players to always play to the very best of their ability. Sometimes, it is a wish to always play even better than they did in their last game. The players who consider themselves their own biggest competition are often the best, smartest players on the court.

The most mentally tough players also need to be able to focus on their game without distractions. Playing in front of a room full of cheering fans can be very distracting, but players and coaches know that the players need to be able to ignore the distractions and focus on the game. Sports psychologists can help basketball players learn to tune out the distractions that a packed arena or gymnasium can provide, and keep their brain on the task at hand: playing strong offense and smart defense.

The toughest players can perform well under pressure. When a player is particularly good on the court, the opposing team will up its defense on that player, which can create a lot of pressure. The Michael Jordans and Kevin Durants of the basketball world have to train their brain to block out the pressure of being heavily guarded by the other team and focus on playing at the top of their ability.

Coaches sometimes sketch out strategies for players to follow on the court.

Playing in front of a big crowd can add stress to a pressure-filled game.

PLANNING THE GAME'S TONE

To prepare a team for a game, a coach must look at the opposing team and decide what the tone of the game should be. In many instances, the coach will already be familiar with the opposing team. The two teams will probably have met previously on the court. The coach can take what they know about the opposing team from past games and use it to build a game strategy.

If the opposing team is new to the coach, the coach can still come up with a strategy and an overall game tone by studying footage of the players in past games. Every good coach will find the weaknesses in the opposing team and its players as individuals. The coach will then devise the team's strategies to break through the other team's weak spots.

Coaches read the game and set the tone for players. Will they emphasize defense or offense? It depends on the strengths of the opposition.

Some teams are aggressive on the offense and run the ball down the court quickly. Other teams focus more on defense and slowing down the opposing team. If a coach is facing an aggressive, offense-heavy team, they will most likely set the tone of the game as defense-heavy. The team's primary goal will be to push back the other team's offense as much as possible and block their openings for shots.

If the coach is facing a team that is strong on defense, they will set the tone of the game as an aggressive, forward-moving one. The coach will encourage the players to move the ball down the court as fast as possible, as often as possible.

Being a coach means working hard to get the best from team players. Smart coaches know that practice may make perfect in a physical sense, but mental strategy is the extra piece that will take a strong team to the next level.

MIND VS. MUSCLE

ALL ABOUT THE DEFENSE

Mike Brown has moved around a lot. He has coached the San Antonio Spurs, Washington Wizards, Indiana Pacers, Cleveland Cavaliers, Los Angeles Lakers, and Golden State Warriors. One thing he learned from more experienced coaches was to hammer defense—drill it into the players over and over. If they had a strong defense, the other team would not be able to score nearly as many points. He was fired from a few coaching positions when his strong defense strategy did not seem to be paying off.

In a losing 2006 game, while he was coaching the Cavaliers, Brown finally threw up his hands near the end of the fourth quarter and told the team to do whatever it wanted. The defense-heavy strategy he had planned was not paying off in that game. That unexpected statement from Brown jolted LeBron James into action, and he rallied the rest of the team to refocus on the defense strategy. The newly energized team went back out on the court, focused on defense, and won the game.

Former Cavaliers coach Mike Brown (right) is known for emphasizing a strong defense.

CHAPTER 4

OFFENSIVE Strategies

Although a strong defense is critical to winning a game, in some ways, offensive strategy is the most important part of the game of basketball. A team can have a terrific defense, but if there is no real offense, that team will score very few points. Great coaches and players know that an offense that combines skill and strategy is vital to a winning team.

Offensive strategy is what allows teams to score.

OFFENSIVE PLAY IN EARLY BASKETBALL

Basketball began as an outdoor sport, which means that the weather was a factor. Any breeze could affect a shot, and a really windy day could make it almost impossible to shoot with accuracy. So, early players focused on shots from short distances. The closer to the hoop a player was when the shot was made, the less likely the player was to be vulnerable to external factors such as wind.

Layups were popular, too, since they were very short-range shots made from just under the hoop. Three-point shots were not nearly as common, because it was hard to control a ball shot from that far from the hoop. Passing was very important in early basketball strategy, too. Coaches knew that short-range shots were going to be the most effective. As a result, they focused their strategy on teaching players how to pass the ball quickly between themselves to get it into the hands of a player located near the hoop.

Early basketball strategy included a lot of passing.

Coaches in these early years of basketball focused greatly on team strategy. They discouraged dribbling because it was a very individual action. Passing was more of a team strategy, and coaches thought it was the best way to move the ball around the court and keep the team working together. In fact, dribbling was so discouraged that in 1920, the New York Celtics supported the rules committee suggestion to make dribbling illegal. Fortunately for today's game, that rule change never happened.

PUMP FAKES

Pump fakes are a simple but very effective offensive strategy. In a pump fake, the offensive player who is holding the ball, fakes a shot without their feet ever leaving the ground. In response, the defensive player will either jump to block the anticipated shot or move to attempt to block the offensive player's motion. Either way, the defensive player is put off guard, which allows the offensive player to make a move.

Pump fakes are used frequently in the NBA. According to Vantage Sports, more than 12 percent of the 6,405 shots taken by NBA players in the 2014–15 season followed pump fakes. Pump fakes also resulted in assists and **turnovers**. The NBA teams that used the most pump fakes prior to shots on the basket for the 2014–15 season were the Chicago Bulls, the Washington Wizards, and the Milwaukee Bucks.

A player from the Temple Owls reacts to a pump fake by the opposing team.

Dwyane Wade makes the pump fake look easy! Pump fakes are simple but effective.

ALL IN THE MIND

Dwyane Wade: King of the Pump Fake

Many consider Dwyane Wade, who played for 13 years for the Miami Heat before moving to the Chicago Bulls in 2016, to be the master of the pump fake. Wade says there is a purely physical aspect to pump fakes, as well as strategy. On the physical side, he says when a defender sees an offensive player move as if to shoot, the defensive player's body will naturally move upward in a jump to block the shot. In a 2009 interview, he said that it was human nature to do this.

However, Wade says that when he is doing a pump fake, he has to read the defensive player. If he knows the defensive player will automatically jump straight up, he will use that knowledge to determine what he will do with the opening he creates from the pump fake. If the defensive player automatically jumps backward, Wade uses a different strategy for the moments after his pump fake. And, Wade adds, even he can be fooled by a pump fake. When playing defense, he has sometimes been caught off guard by an offensive player using a pump fake on him.

SCREENS

In the early 1900s, teams used a lot of **man-to-man defense**, which was fairly effective when used against passing, short-range shots, and layups. Coaches found a way around the man-to-man defense with a strategy known as a **screen**. In a screen, the offensive player stands behind or beside a defender and essentially forms a wall that another offensive player can run behind to "lose" the defensive player, who is supposed to be covering the offensive player. That leaves the offensive player open to take a shot when the ball is passed. It is a simple but brilliant strategy that is still used today.

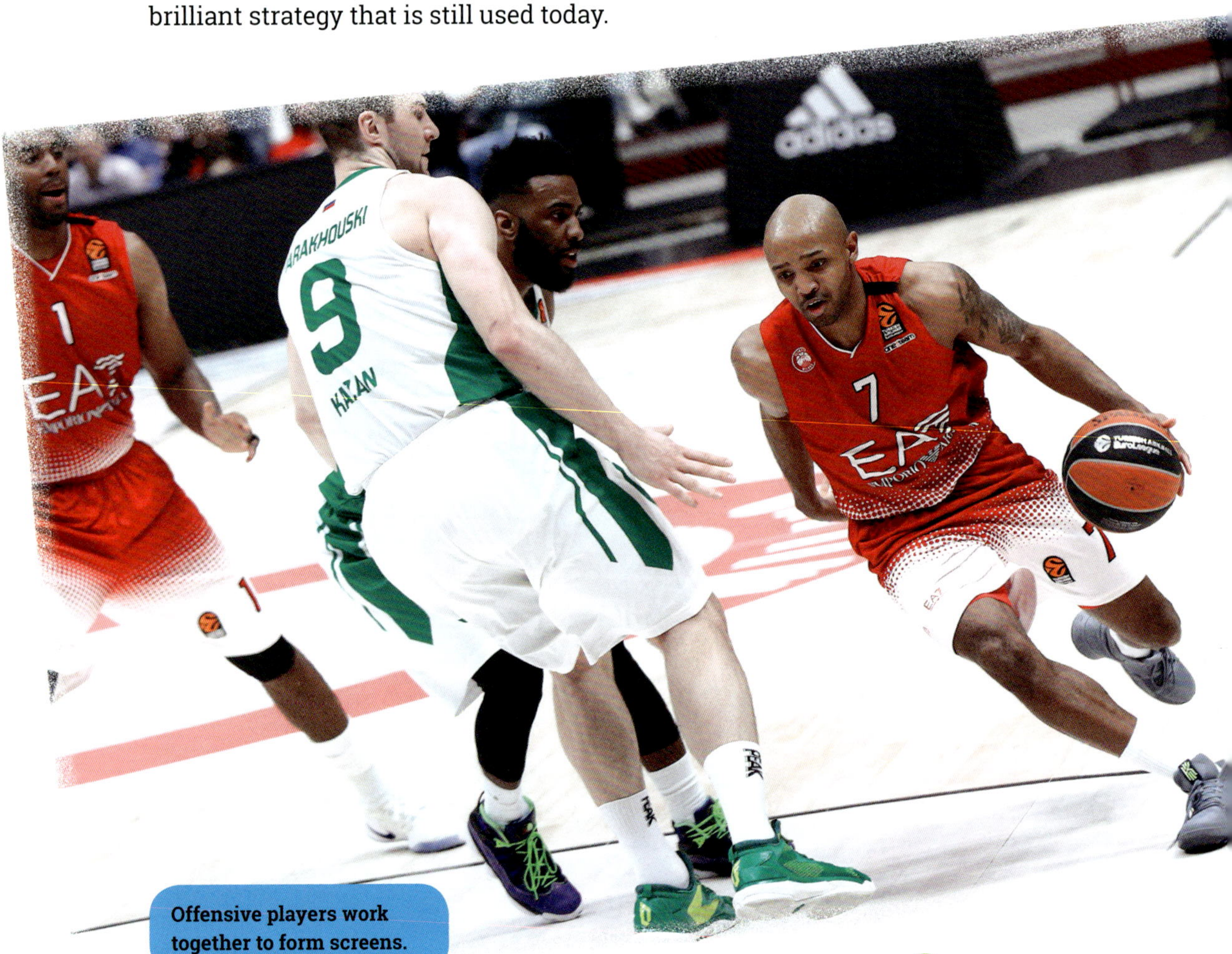

Offensive players work together to form screens.

Even a foul shot can provide the opposing team with a chance to take control of the ball and ultimately score.

MIND VS. MUSCLE

TURNING NEGATIVE INTO POSITIVE: FOUL-SHOT REBOUNDS

Not every basketball player is going to be a great foul shooter. A smart team can turn this negative into a positive.

Fouls happen all the time in basketball. Over the last 35 years, the average number of fouls in a college basketball game has ranged from 17 to 21. That is an average of about one foul every two minutes! Clearly, foul shots are a big part of basketball games.

If a team has a weak foul shooter, this can be turned into a positive by working on the team's offensive rebound strategy. The offensive rebound strategy can be any of a number of types—the point is to find ones that play to the team's strengths and then work on them in practice.

Coaches and players can use the sports psychology technique of goal setting as they practice their offensive rebound strategies. In goal setting, an athlete or team sets small, measurable goals that they can work on to eventually meet a longer-term goal. In this case, the long-term goal might be, "We want 75 percent of all missed foul shots to result in offensive opportunities, rather than turnovers." The shorter-term goals might be smaller pieces, such as, "We want at least two missed foul shots in next week's game to result in offensive opportunities."

An added bonus to turning this negative into a positive is that it may also take some pressure off of the foul shooter. That player's foul shooting may improve, simply because they know that if they miss the shot, the stakes are not so high. His teammates will take an offensive opportunity even if he misses.

CHAPTER 5

DEFENSIVE Strategies

While offensive strategy is crucial for scoring points, defensive strategy is also an incredibly important part of basketball. If a team is weak on defense, it will be no match for the opponents. On a basketball team, players must play both offense and defense. They may be skilled shooters or excellent at assists, but they must also know defensive strategy.

EARLY DEFENSIVE SKILLS AND STRATEGIES

Up until about the 1920s, coaches based their strategy on defense. Many coaches used a man-to-man defensive strategy, where each defensive player was to keep one offensive player from scoring. So many of the early offensive plays were short-range shots that it made sense to focus on defense.

Defensive coverage is generally either zone or man-to-man.

If an offensive player was given an opening for a short-range shot, it was likely that the player would make the basket. The defense's entire purpose was to keep the other team from scoring, so they had to concentrate on not letting the offensive players get the chance to shoot.

When offensive strategies became more complicated, using screens and set plays, coaches had to switch to defensive strategies other than the straight man-to-man defense. Teams needed to be able to defend against longer-range shots, which were becoming more common. They also needed to defend against dribbling, which was becoming a more common way to move the ball around on the court.

In the mid-1930s and early 1940s, teams began switching to **zone defense**. In this type of defense, each defender covers a particular part of the basketball court, instead of covering one specific player. Zone defense forced offensive players into taking more outside shots, since the inside zones were heavily guarded. These shots were more difficult than short-range shots, and so the offense was less likely to make a basket on them.

Various types of zone defense began to be used later in basketball. But in the early days of the game, it was generally straight man-to-man defense or straight zone defense.

Man-to-man defense was the most popular defensive strategy in early basketball, and it is still used today.

MIND VS. MUSCLE

DEFENDING SMART

Andre Iguodala is known as one of the best defenders in the NBA. In his mind, sometimes defense is more about how you do not play someone than how you do. LeBron James is an intimidating offensive player. He is fast, he is large, and he is a tremendous athlete. The two came face to face in a game where the Miami Heat (with James) took on the Denver Nuggets (with Iguodala). Iguodala knew that if he charged James when James had the ball, Iguodala would get the foul. He also knew that getting hit by James would be like being run over by a truck. So, instead of an obvious defense, he moved backward as James approached him, and he set his mind to distracting James, so that James could not get a clear shot. It worked beautifully.

Andre Iguodala's athleticism and tactical play make him one of the best defenders in the game.

HACK-A-SHAQ

Hack-a-Shaq is quite a smart defensive strategy that capitalizes on particular players' weaknesses. If a team is having a particularly strong offensive game, but it has one player who is a weak free throw shooter, the losing team may use that to its advantage. Instead of continuing traditional game play and allowing the offensive team to continue scoring, the losing team will sometimes repeatedly commit personal fouls against a weak free throw shooter on the winning team. This results in the weak shooter repeatedly taking (and likely missing) free throws and the losing team regaining control of the ball.

The name of this strategy came from strategy against Shaquille O'Neal, who was a powerful (and exceptionally large) player, but who was known to be weak on the free throw line. Opposing teams who were losing would repeatedly foul Shaq, forcing him into taking free throws that he was not necessarily likely to make. However, Shaq was not the first player this strategy was used against. Chicago Bulls power forward Dennis Rodman was similarly weak at free throws, and it is reported that the strategy was devised for use when opposing teams were losing to Rodman's team.

The Hack-a-Shaq strategy was named for player Shaquille O'Neal's somewhat dismal free-throw ability.

CONFUSING THE OFFENSE: JUNK DEFENSE

Sometimes, the smartest strategies are the simplest. If a team is facing an opposing team that has a really strong offensive player, possibly the best thing is to try to tire out and distract that player. One way to do so is by using **junk defenses**. Junk defenses are nontraditional defense strategies that are designed to confuse the offense, among other things.

A junk defense can be a risky strategy because it can leave holes open on the court, opening up lanes for shooting and driving. However, it can also be a smart strategy because it can confuse the offensive players who have spent time practicing against more traditional man-to-man and zone defense strategies. Confusion is tiring for players; so is having to make extra moves on the court that they were not expecting because they were faced with a surprising defense. The opposing team's star player may get out of their usual playing rhythm when faced with junk defenses.

If a game is not going well, a team may resort to using junk defenses to tire out their opponents.

Coaches will sketch out the strategy for players before the game and during time-outs.

Using a junk defense against a team with a particular star player is a common defensive strategy. The smartest teams will use a junk defense that tires out the other team's star not only on offense, but also on defense—when the team has control of the ball, it will force the opposing team's star into playing defense to tire out the player and make the offense less effective. If the team is able to force the star player to play defense, that player is less of a threat than if they consistently stay in the half of the court near the team's basket. In this instance, if the star player does gain control of the ball, they have to move much farther down the court to make a basket when the player has been pressed to fall back on defense.

One way that coaches can help prepare their teams to use junk defense is by using self-talk. Self-talk is a set of thoughts and phrases that athletes can say to themselves to prepare for a specific type of play. If coaches work with their team on a self-talk phrase to use when using a junk defense on the court, it can help the team relax into the unfamiliar play.

CHAPTER 6

GAME-DAY Ready!

It all comes down to the big game. Everything players have worked toward goes into this day. The best players will have spent countless hours doing physical drills and practice to hone their athleticism on the court. They will also have used mental strategies to get ready for the game. When the coach says, "Get your mind in the game," they are ready to do just that.

Indiana Hoosiers coach Bob Knight has been quoted as saying that the ratio of mental to physical in prepping for the game is 4:1—in other words, playing a good game is four parts mental strength and one part athleticism. Others have gone so far as to say that the game of basketball is 90 percent mental and 10 percent physical. With that in mind, it is clear that the best players will find mental strategies to help them get in the right mind-set for play.

Teams work hard to psych themselves up for the big game.

PREPARING FOR THE BIG GAME

The most effective mental strategies to prepare for the big game vary from player to player, but there are many to choose from.

Don't Think Too Much

Players and coaches spend hours analyzing their play: their defense, their shooting, their passing, their dribbling. However, when the big day comes, one very effective strategy is to stop thinking. Games are fast-paced and not the best time to analyze the mechanics of play. When players see an opening to shoot, many coaches will say they should shoot—not take a second to analyze how to shoot. That should have been done before the game, and there is plenty of time for it to be done after the game, too, to improve the player's future game play. In the heat of the game, do not think—just play.

There is no time to stop and think during a fast-paced game. Players need to play from their gut.

Focus on Success, Not Failure

In basketball, everyone misses shots. No one has a perfect shooting record—or even close to one. Worrying about missed shots creates an anxiety that will only limit the players' game.

Rather than focusing on missed shots, players can keep their head in the game by focusing on what they do well. If they are having an off game for shooting, they can focus on defense.

Clear Out Mental Clutter

Some players talk about being in "the zone," where their thinking is clear and focused on the goal at hand. They do not hear the crowd, they do not hear cheers or boos. They are not thinking about worries they may have had before the game or whatever they need to do after the game. They are simply in the zone, focused on playing the game.

Players can use different methods to clear out mental clutter. Some like to make lists of things they need to accomplish outside the game, so they can stop focusing on these during the game. Others use relaxation

Players all have different strategies for blocking out the noise and getting rid of mental clutter before a game.

Although players want to relax before a game, they also do not want to become too relaxed—they need energy to perform on the court!

techniques or meditation. Still others find that certain songs or types of music help them get into the zone. Whatever helps a player clear the clutter and get in the zone is an effective mental strategy to prepare for the big game.

Being Comfortable with Discomfort

There is no doubt about it—games are not always comfortable. There are distractions. There is competition. There is pressure to perform well. Games are fun, but they can also be uncomfortable.

To increase players' mental toughness on the court, coaches recommend that they learn to become comfortable with being uncomfortable. There is no way to avoid the discomfort, so they help players embrace it. Players are encouraged to focus on what they can control, stay in the zone as much as possible—and know that there will be times when they are distinctly uncomfortable.

One way to be comfortable with discomfort is for players to understand the things that they can and cannot control. Players can control their focus, their attitude, their effort, their communication on the court (verbal and nonverbal), and their thoughts. They cannot control the spectators, the referees, or the opposing team.

ALL IN THE MIND

Steph Curry: Mental Training for the Big Game

Steph Curry has been an undisputed star in recent NBA championships, leading the Golden State Warriors to two championship wins over a three-year span. He is thought to be one of the greatest shooters in basketball history. In 2017, he spoke to health-care giant Kaiser Permanente about the mental strategies he uses to prepare for big games. Curry uses a **sensory deprivation chamber**, known as the pod, to help him focus, calm his mind, and prepare for important games. Curry says it is important to block out the noise of negative commentary (which every celebrity is subject to) and focus on playing the best game you can, and the pod helps him do just that.

He also says he likes to be a step ahead in terms of visualizing the game ahead of him, and the focus and calm he achieves enables him to visualize the game and push his play to the next level.

Steph Curry uses sensory deprivation to help calm his mind before a game, and he uses visualization to help him achieve his peak game performance.

Basketball players can visualize themselves flying through the air to make the perfect slam dunk.

Challenge Yourself

Inner motivation is an important characteristic of the best players. They are not motivated by factors such as fame or money. Instead, they are motivated to constantly better their own game and improve their skills.

One way to keep a strong inner motivation is to continually identify areas for improvement and try to better them. Players can identify a weakness in their own play and constantly challenge themselves to improve upon it.

Michael Jordan, widely thought to be one of the greatest basketball players, used this strategy to prepare himself for games. He would dig deep inside himself to identify his weaknesses on the court and then work hard during every game to improve them. Despite knowing that no player can achieve a perfect game, Jordan says he would mentally challenge himself to play a perfect basketball game.

Focus on the Next Play

Looking at a whole game, with many factors out of a player's control, can be overwhelming. Instead, coaches will encourage players to focus on the next play. They want players to move on from the previous play (there is always time to analyze it after the game) and focus completely on the play ahead of them. When that play is complete, then they can move on to the next one. By taking the game one play at a time, players can better keep their focus on the immediate task at hand.

Use Affirmations

Many people believe that if you hear something often enough, you start to believe it. This is true in basketball, too, as it relates to building confidence. Self-confidence is an important characteristic in strong players, and one way to build self-confidence is by using affirmations. Players can practice saying, "I am a great basketball player," or "I am the best shooter on my team," or "I am a strong defender."

Strong players are always looking ahead to the next play.

Players may use affirmations to help prepare for pressure-filled situations, such as shooting free throws.

Psychotherapist Ron Alexander suggests speaking affirmations out loud each day. He says the mind does not always know the difference between what is real and what is fantasy, so if a person repeats an affirmation often enough, their mind will begin to accept it as true. This can then increase the person's self-confidence.

Emphasize Process, Not Product

Players who want to develop mental **resilience** should focus on the process, not the end result. Obviously, the end result anyone desires is a game win. However, teams that focus on the actual win may not be as successful as teams that focus on the characteristics a team needs to be a winner. That is, the players on the team can focus on communicating well as a team, cooperating on the court, emphasizing their strengths, and compensating for weaknesses. If they focus on what makes a winning team, rather than focusing on the win itself, they may find that their game play is much stronger.

A GAME OF WITS

As in any team sport, basketball is made up of many offensive and defensive strategies. Speed on the court is a great asset. Size can be intimidating and used to an advantage in both offense and defense. Even more important for a winning team is understanding offensive and defensive strategies and using the brains of the team to put those strategies into play. Each player must use mental strategies to develop and refine their focus, toughness, and resilience on the court.

Coaches often put together several mental strategies to help their team play the best game possible.

Basketball is a game of speed and size, but it is also a game of wits. The offense constantly has to look for holes in defense and strategize the best way to get an open shot. Meanwhile, the defense has to be sure to cover all zones of the court, leaving no holes for the offense to punch through. Any number of different strategies helps teams do these things well. The trick is having a smart team and coach who can find the best strategies to help the team win the game. Teams also need to know that a loss one day can be a win the next, if players just use their mind to turn it around.

BUILDING AN UNBEATABLE FORCE

The best coaches will inspire their players to adopt that same mind-set. Losses happen, but what is important is getting back in the game and using one's mind to play better and smarter the next time the team steps out on the court. With athleticism, mental focus and strength, strong leadership, and strong team communication, a team can become an unbeatable force on the court. Teams have come back from the bottom of the league and gone on to win championships in later years. A large part of successes like these is the effort the coach and players put into improving their mental game, as well as their physical game.

Basketball is about strategy, mental toughness, and athleticism. Together, these characteristics make a strong player.

GLOSSARY

athleticism strength, fitness, and agility in an athlete

factors facts that contribute to a result or outcome

home team the team that is playing on their home court, in the city or region they represent

goal setting setting small and manageable goals to achieve an overall greater goal

junk defenses informal defense strategies designed to distract offensive players from their routine

layups shots where the player leaps from right below the basket and uses one hand to bounce the ball off the backboard and into the hoop

man-to-man defense a defense strategy in which each player is assigned to guard one other player

mental agility mental quickness or sharpness

mental state state of mind

mental strategy plans to help someone meet a goal

motivational climate the strategy of motivation a coach uses for a team. Motivational climates can be positive, congratulating players on good plays, or negative, berating them for poor plays.

MVP acronym for most valuable player: the standout player on a team

personality traits characteristics of a person's personality

psychiatrist a medical doctor who specializes in mental health

psychology the study of the mind and its functions

rehabilitation recovery from illness or injury

resilience the ability to recover quickly from difficult situations or circumstances

screen a strategy where an offensive player creates a "screen" for a teammate to go around or behind, opening themselves up for a pass and/or shot

self-talk words or phrases a person says to themselves to be more effective in reaching a goal

sensory deprivation chamber a chamber in which a person is deprived of external stimuli. This allows the person to focus more closely on what's in his or her mind.

turnover when a team loses possession to the other team

zone defense a defense strategy in which each player is assigned to guard a particular zone on the court

FOR MORE INFORMATION

BOOKS

LeBoutillier, Nate. *Play Basketball Like a Pro: Key Skills and Tips.* Mankato, MN: Capstone Press, 2011.

Norwich, Grace. *I Am LeBron James.* New York, NY: Scholastic Paperbacks, 2014.

Sports Illustrated Kids. *Big Book of Who: Basketball.* New York, NY: Sports Illustrated Kids, 2015.

Sports Illustrated Kids. *Slam Dunk! Top 10 Lists of Everything in Basketball.* New York, NY: Sports Illustrated Kids, 2014.

WEBSITES

Watch a movie and take a basketball quiz with BrainPop Sports and Fitness at:
www.brainpop.com/health/sportsandfitness

Find out more about basketball at:
www.ducksters.com/sports/basketball.php

Read about your favorite NBA players and teams at:
jr.nba.com

Read the online Sports Illustrated magazine especially for younger readers at:
www.sikids.com

INDEX